HIEROGLYPHIC

Origin of
ABCs
for Children and Big Kids

RICH AMENINHAT

Erika Goodkin-Domingue, Consulting Editor,
Literati Consulting Public Relations

Copyright © 2022 by Rich Ameninhat

All rights reserved. No part of this publication may be reproduced, distributed, or transmitted in any form or by any means, including photocopying, recording, or other electronic or mechanical methods, without the prior written permission of the publisher, except in the case of brief quotations embodied in critical reviews and certain other noncommercial uses permitted by copyright law. For permission requests, write to the publisher, addressed "Attention: Permissions Coordinator," at:

Ameninhat@gmail.com

Printed in the United States of America
Books may be ordered through bookseller
Amazon.com

First Printing: 2017, 2022
ISBN 978-0996906661
All rights reserved.

DEDICATION

To my daughter, Kylene TIRAET, L-Earn My dear! There is gr8ness in U to share world-'round. Love to you always

and

Great Grandfather Elliot Singleton; Your deep spiritual legacy, that of our Ancestors', lives on.

CONTENT:

*The Origin of Alphabet, ABCs

*The Hieroglyphs I shared with/ "taught" Kylene Tiraet, when she was 4-years-old

*Appendix

x

INTRODUCTION

With look of concern and deep confusion she said, "Please... Please... I want to understand. Now, can you explain it to me like I'm a five-year-old?"

Why is the sky blue? What is the importance of <u>The Tao of Poo</u> and <u>Te of Piglet</u>?

Those are seemingly simple and at the same time can be lifelong questions to answer.

Parsimony, the essentially simple and full filling "way to go" comes to mind.

This will be the standard of this book. Not to skirt around the topic nor assume or demean the reader's understanding, this approach in essence is best, penultimate.

For others who want, need or demand a more technical scholarly presentation with all the bells and whistles and more, there is a complimentary adult book HD Hieroglyphic Definitives, by Rich Ameninhat.

This book will be parsimonious at every twist and turn, with corresponding page suggested activities at the back, Appendix, of the book for each main point.

It is recommend for teaching purposes that the Appendix be read prior to sharing with youngsters and others.

Generally structured ([D., E., F.] Discussion topic, Exercise, Fun Facts), this can be expanded or contracted to meet which ever scholastic level or goal.

For ever blessed, may this work expand the horizon of yours and whomever interacts with it directly or indirectly.

Amenet Amef Amen: It is, so let it be so.

From WHERE do ABCs come?

This is Our Planet:

This is a Map of Our World:

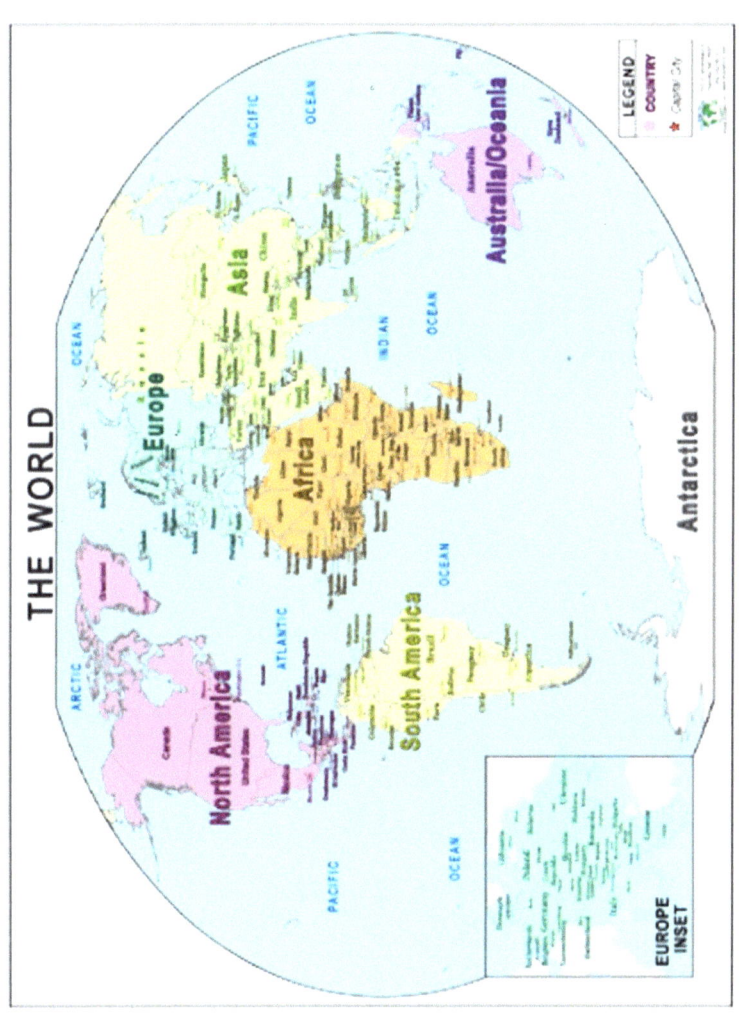

From WHERE Do ABCs come?

Like Hansel and Gretel's Breadcrumbs,

We can follow a trail to find out:

The Arrow points to Russia:

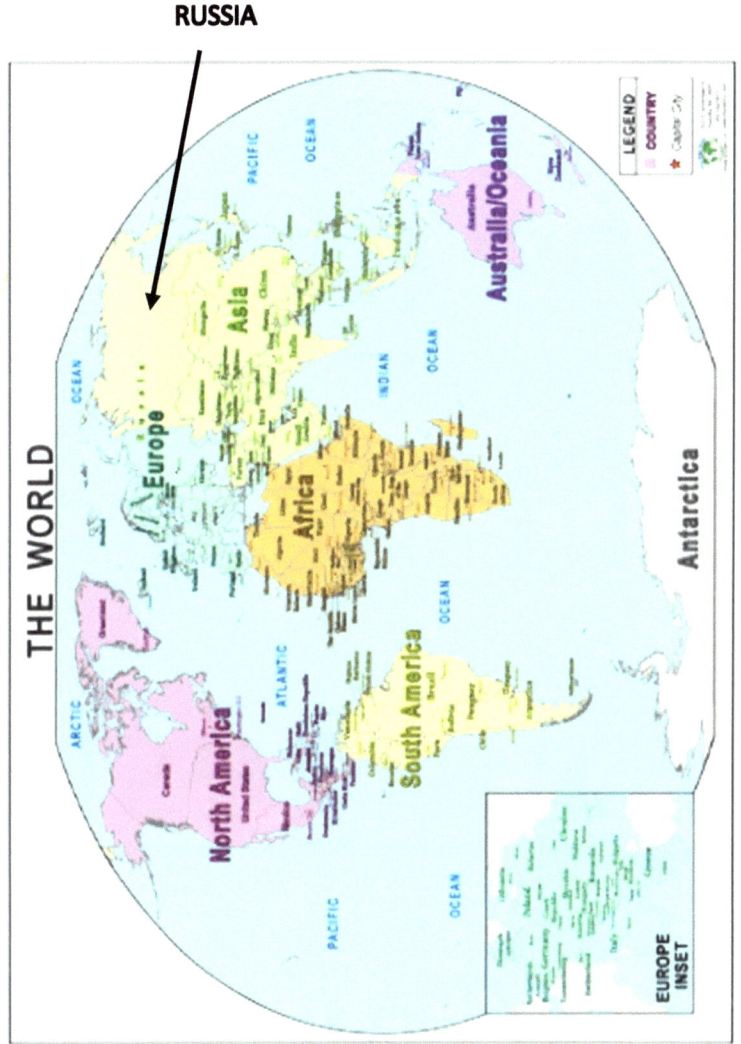

Russia has one of the <u>youngest</u> ABCs:

Russian ABCs

А	Б	В	Г	Д	Е
Ё	Ж	З	И	Й	К
Л	М	Н	О	П	Р
С	Т	У	Ф	Х	Ц
Ч	Ш	Щ	Ъ	Ы	Ь
Э	Ю	Я			

Origin around 800 PE (Present Era, The present), CE, or AD.

It Looks

Almost

Exactly like

COPTIC

ABCs:

Coptic ABCs:
Is older and has more letters than Russian and Greek

No one is **Sure**, but Coptic is from about 2 - 1000 BPE (Before Present Era), BCE, or BC.

COPTIC and RUSSIAN

COPTIC LETTERS	NAMES OF COPTIC LETTERS		"ENGLISH" PHONETIC VALUE	Russian Letters
ⲁ	Alpha	ⲁⲗⲫⲁ	a	А а (A)
ⲃ	Bida	ⲃⲓⲇⲁ	b	Б б (B)/В в (V)
ⲅ	Gamma	ⲅⲁⲙⲙⲁ	g	Г г (G)
ⲇ	Dalda	ⲇⲁⲗⲇⲁ	d	Д д (D)
ⲉ	Ei	ⲉⲓ	e	Е е (E) Э э
				Ё ё (YO) (Ë)
ⲍ	Zita	ⲍⲓⲧⲁ	z	З з (Z)/Ж ж (ZH)
ⲏ	Êta	ⲏⲧⲁ	ê	Й й (Y)
ⲑ	Thita	ⲑⲓⲧⲁ	th	Ъ (-)
ⲓ	Iauta	ⲓⲁⲩⲧⲁ	i	И и (I) {Ы (Y) Ь (')}
ⲕ	Kappa	ⲕⲁⲡⲡⲁ	k	К к (K)
ⲗ	Laula	ⲗⲁⲩⲗⲁ	l	Л л (L)
ⲙ	Mi	ⲙⲓ	m	М м (M)
ⲛ	Ni	ⲛⲓ	n	Н н (N)
ⲝ	Xi	ⲝⲓ	x (ks)	
ⲟ	O	ⲟ	o	О о (O)
ⲡ	Pi	ⲡⲓ	p	П п (P)
ⲣ	Ro	ⲣⲟ	r	Р р (R)
ⲥ	Sima	ⲥⲓⲙⲁ	s	С с (S)
ⲧ	Tau	ⲧⲁⲩ	t	Т т (T)
ⲩ	Ue	ⲩⲉ	u, y	У у (U)
ⲫ	Phi	ⲫⲓ	ph	
ⲭ	Chi	ⲭⲓ	kh	Х х (KH)
ⲯ	Psi	ⲯⲓ	ps	Ц ц (TS)
ⲱ	Au (O)	ⲱⲩ	ô	{Ю (YU or IU) Я (YA or IA)}
ϣ	Shei	ϣⲉⲓ	sh	Ш ш (SH)
ϥ	Fei	ϥⲉⲓ	f	Ф ф (F)
ϧ	Chei (Xei)	ϧⲉⲓ	ch	Ч ч (CH)
ϩ	Hori	ϩⲟⲣⲓ	h	
ϫ	Djandjia	ϫⲁⲛϫⲓⲁ	dj	
ϭ	Tchima	ϭⲓⲙⲁ	tch	Щ щ (SHCH)
ϯ	Ti	ϯ	ti (di)	

From WHERE does COPTIC come?:

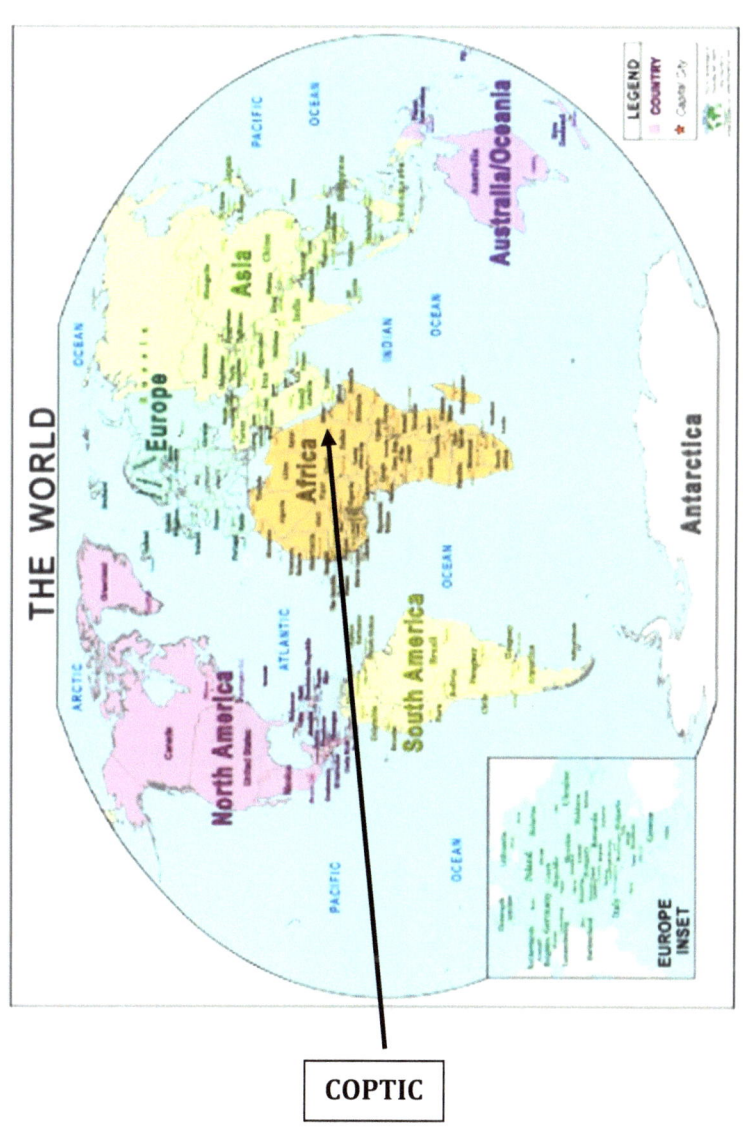

What or who is Coptic???

They are people originally directly related to

Ancient Egyptians (Chemit), <u>origin</u> from 4–10,000± BCE.

The Rosetta Stone from Chemit had *Breadcrumbs* to translate Hieroglyphics:

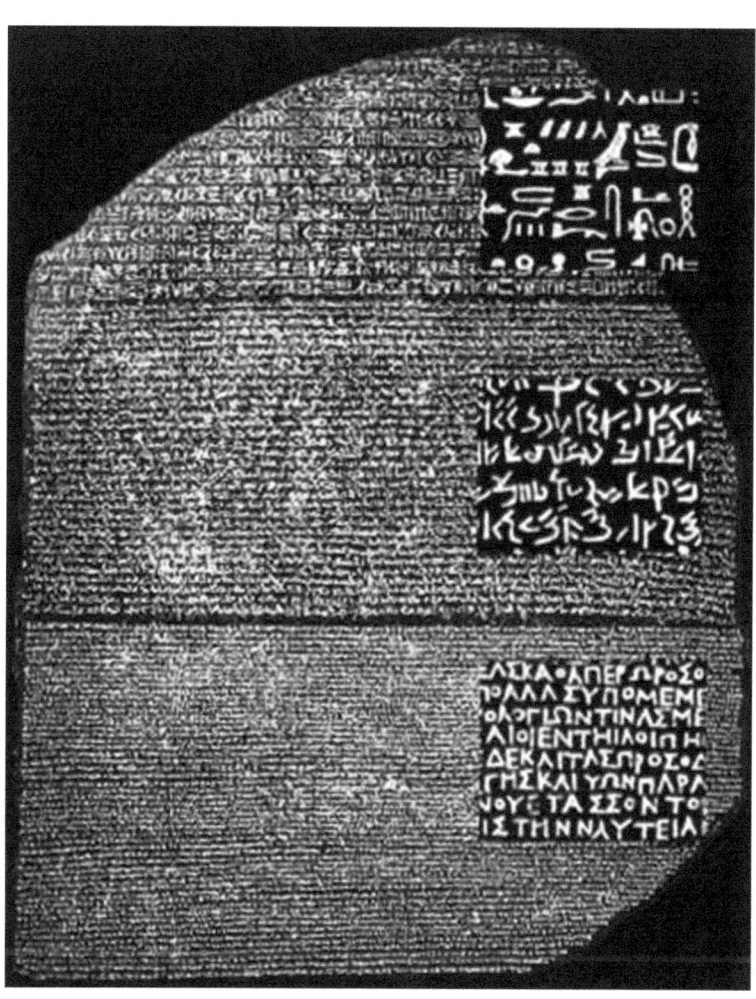

Jean François Champollion used

COPTIC

to

Decipher

the Stone:

Champollion's work and study of Hieroglyphics Helped connect "ABC Breadcrumbs":

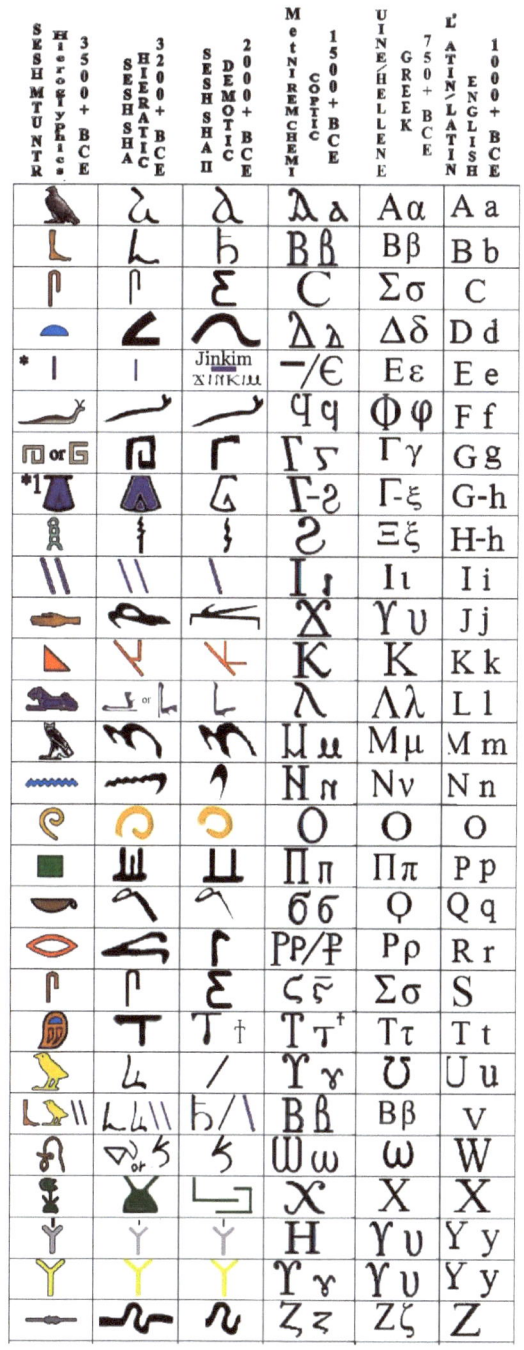

Coptic also looks almost exactly like Greek:

GREEK

Coptic, Greek, Hebrew, Arabic... even have almost the same names for ABCs:

Hieroglyphs to Stick-figure Glyphs Names A-Z

	Rem Chemi (Ancient Egyptian)	Ni Rem Chemi (Coptic "dialect")	Canaanite, Hebrew ("Phoenician")	Uine [Ooiney], Hellene (Greek)	Arabah (Arabic)	
A a	Akham, Alhoum-Axum…	Akham, Alhoum- Axum…	Aleph	Alpha	Alif
B b	Bata, Beta, Bita…	Bida	Beth	Beta	Ba`
C	Es, Se[h]	Sima, Seema	Sin	Sigma	Sin
D d	Da, De, Di…	Dalda	Daleth	Delta	Dal
E e	Eh	Ei	Ayin+	Epsilon	Ayn
F f	Fa, Fe, Fi… or Af, Ef, If…	Fe	Peh, Phe	Phi	Fa
G g	Ga, Ge, Gi…	Ghamma	Gimel	Gamma	Gim
H h	Heh	Hori	Hê	Heta	Ha
I i	Ih	Iauta	Iódh	Iota	Ya`, Aye (Eye)
J	Ja, Je, Ji…	Djandi	Gimel	Gamma	Jim, Gim
K	Ka, Ke, Ki…	Kabba	Koph	Kappa	Kaf
L l	La, Le, Li…	Laula	Lamedh	Lambda	Lam
M m	Ma, Me, Mi… (Mu)	Mi	Mem	Mu	Mim
N n	Na, Ne, Ni… (Nu)	Ni	Nun	Nu	Nun
O	Ouh, Oh	O	Vav, Ah	Omicron	Ha, Ah
P p	Pa, Pe, Pi…	Pi	Peh	Pi	Ba, Pa or Pe
Q q	Qa, Qe, Qi…	Qeema	Kof	Qoppa	Qaf
R r	Ar, Ee, Ir…, Ra, Re, Ri…	Ro, Ra, Re…	Resh	Rho	Ra`
S	Es, Se[h]	Sima, Seema	Sin	Sigma	Sin
T t	Tau, Ta	Tau	Teth	Tau	Ta
U u	Ū (OO)	Ū	Wâw	O[Uh]mega	Waw, Damma
V	Fa, Fe, Fi…	Fa… or Bida- Ū	Vav	Beta	Ve (Fa/ two dots)
W	Wah, Ūa (Ooah, Wahl)	Wah, Ūa	Wâw	Uhmega-Alpha	Waw
X	Xi	Xi	Kôf-Sin	Xi	Kâf-sin
Y y	Yâau, Yâaut…	Eey/Ē, [H]ē, H ē	Iodh-ayin	Ypsilon/Upsil.	Ya`, Aida
Z	Zeh	Zita	Zayin	Zeta	Sâd, Zâd, Za

Some think **Hebrew did** not "directly" come from **Hieroglyphics** but in 1813 PE Wilhelm *Gesenius* **proved them** wrong:

Gesenius' Hebrew
ABCs Chart

Some think that **Phoenician** did not come from **Chemit,** but the older Hieroglyphics and younger ABCs look the same, and **Chemit** and **Phoenicia** was a close neighbor:

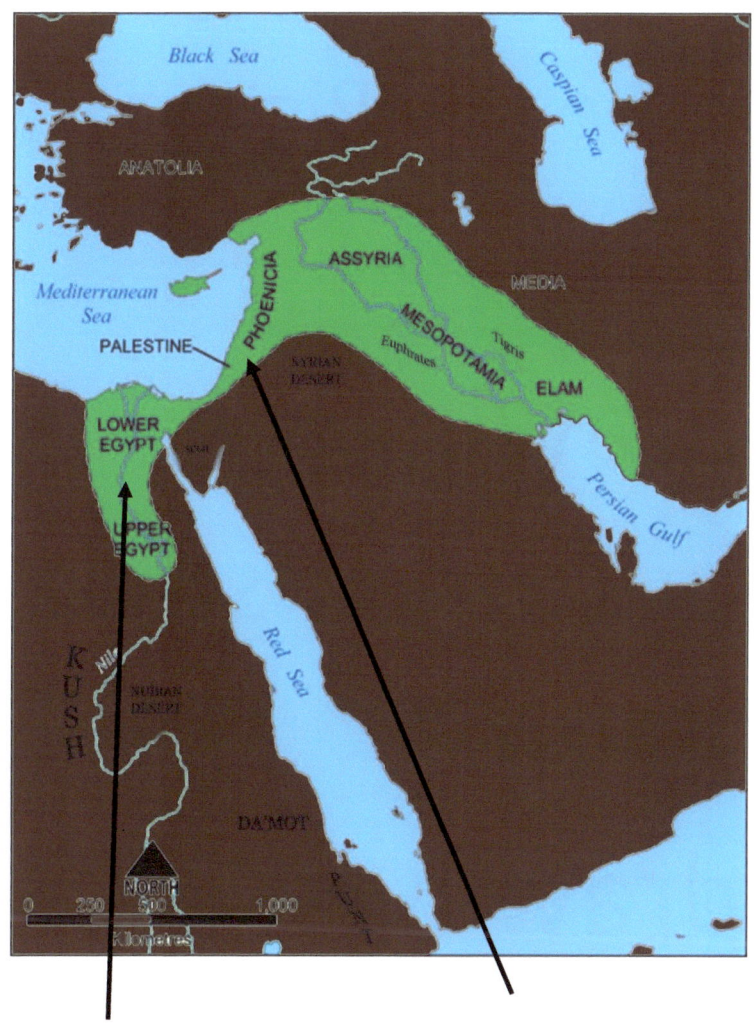

Chemit   Phoenicia

It's Simple and makes sense to Little and Big Kids...

Detailed drawings became "stick figure" drawings:

Mm

q Q

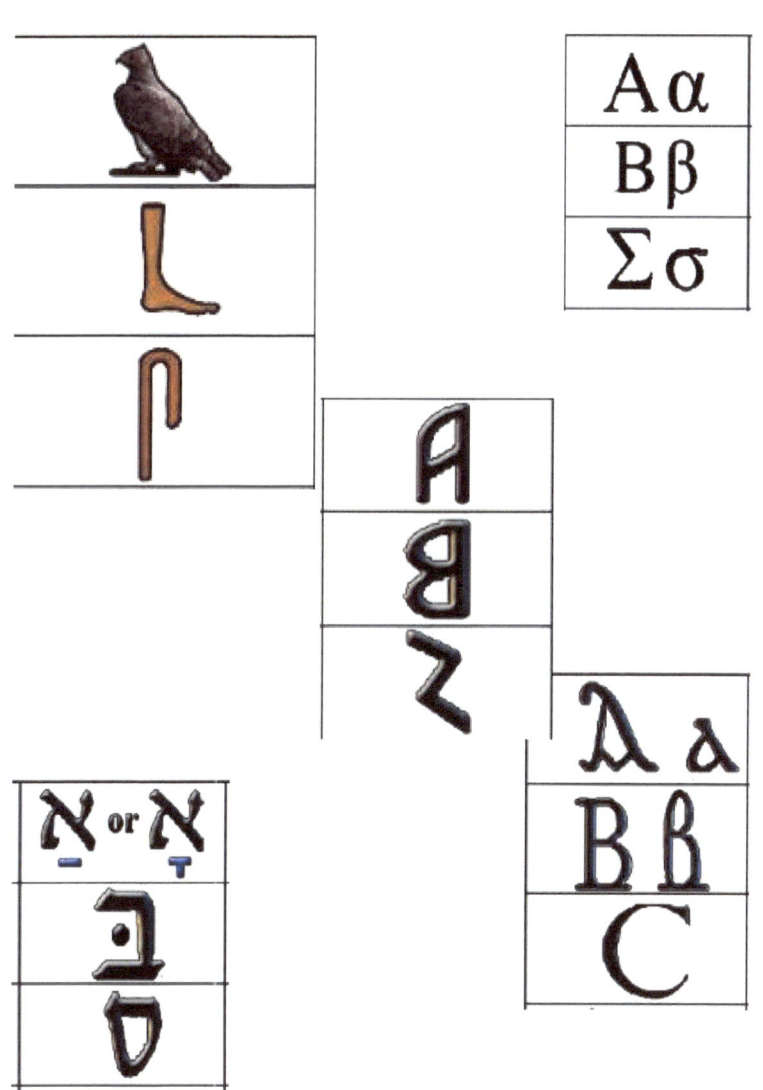

SEE?

ABCs - 7000+ Years of EVOLUTION Worldwide

SESH MTUNTR Hieroglyphics 3500+ BCE	SESH HIERATIC SHA 3200+ BCE	SESH DEMOTIC SHAI II 2000+ BCE	Metnirem Chemi COPTIC 1500+ BCE	KANANA/CANAAN PHOENICIAN 1500+ BCE	RASNA ETRUSCAN 1000+ BCE	UINE HELLEN GREEK 750+ BCE E	Hapiru/IVRIT HEBREW 135- CE	AL ARABYAH ARABIC 650- CE	L' ATIN/LATIN ENGLISH 1000+ BCE
🦅	ȃ	ג	Ⲁ a	A	A	Αα	א or אַ	ا	A a
👣	L	ƅ	B β	P	8	Ββ	ב	ب	B b
⌐	⌐	Σ	C	5	ʒ	Σσ	ד	ش	C
●	∠	∠	Δ λ	D	⊲	Δδ	٦	כ	D d
∣ and —	∣ and —	Jinkim / ΧΠΚΙΜ	ⲉ/Є	E	⊒	Εε	אֶ	ع	E e
~	~	~	Ϥ ϥ	F	⊒	Φφ	פ	ف	F f
ⓂorⒼ	𐌂	Γ	Γ ɣ	Γ	⊃	Γγ	ג	ج	G g
*1	▲	⌐	Γ-ϛ	Γ-Β	⊃-Β	Γ-ξ	ה	غ	G-h
⅄	∮	∮	ⲋ	Θ	Θ	Ξξ	ה	ح	H-h
\\	\\	\	I ι	I	I	Ιι	א	\	I i
🍶	🐦	⌐	X	|	|	Υυ	'	ج	J j
▲	↓	↓	Κ	Κ	X	Κ	כ	ك	K k
🐆	∟	∟	λ	L	L	Λλ	ל	J	L l
𓂝	𓂧	𓂧	Μ μ	M	M	Μμ	מ	م	M m
﹏﹏	⌒⌒	⌒	Η ɲ	ᒥ	ᒥ	Νν	נ	ن	N n
◉	◯	◯	O	O	O	O	א	ه	O
▪	𐰢	𐰢	Π π	Γ	ᒍ	Ππ	פ	ب	P p
⟟	⟟	⟟	ϭ ϭ	Ϙ	Ϙ	Ϙ	ק	ق	Q q
◇	⟟	⟟	Ⲣⲣ/Ᵽ	P	ᑫ	Ρρ	ר	ل	R r
⌐	⌐	∑	ϛ ϛ̄	ς	⌐	Σσ	⊽ and ש	ش	S
▼	T	T	Τ τ	T	T	Ττ	v and ת	ت	T t
🐦	⌐	/	Υ ɣ	V	V	Υ	·	و	U u
𐤋𐤋\\	⌐⌐\\	ƅ/\\	Β β	P	8	Ββ	ב	ف	V
𓆑	⌑⌑ϟ	ϟ	Ш ω	W	W	ω	ו	و	W
✚	✚	⌐	ⲭ	X	X	X	ϭϭ	س ك	X
ψ	ψ	ψ	H	Y	Y	Υυ	אֶ	ئ	Y y
Ψ	Ψ	Ψ	Υ ɣ	Y	Y	Υυ	'	ئ	Y y
—	~	~	Ζ ζ	Ƨ	ϟ	Ζζ	ז	ذ, ظ	Z

© 2022 RICH AMENINHAT

Now We Know the Origin of ABCs...

Please Tell a Friend to read with Me.

Some Hieroglyphs and ABCs I shared with/"taught" Kylene Tiraet when she was 4-years-old

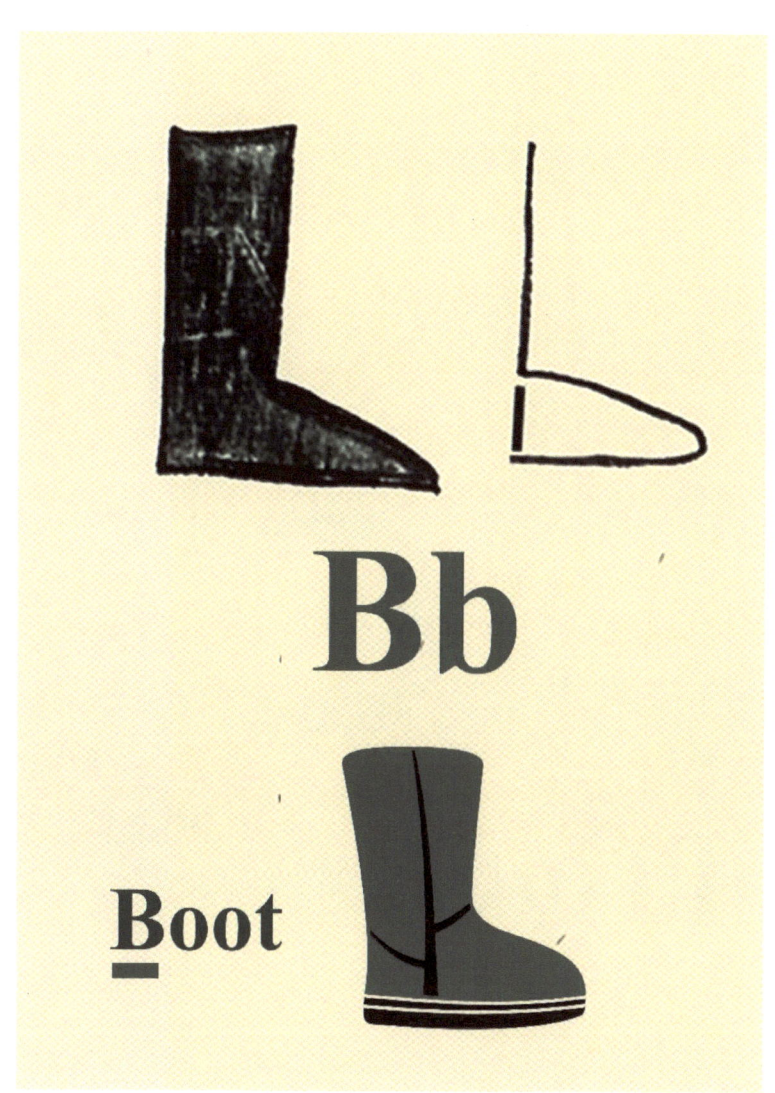

Bb

Boot

C

Prin<u>c</u>essa

Donut

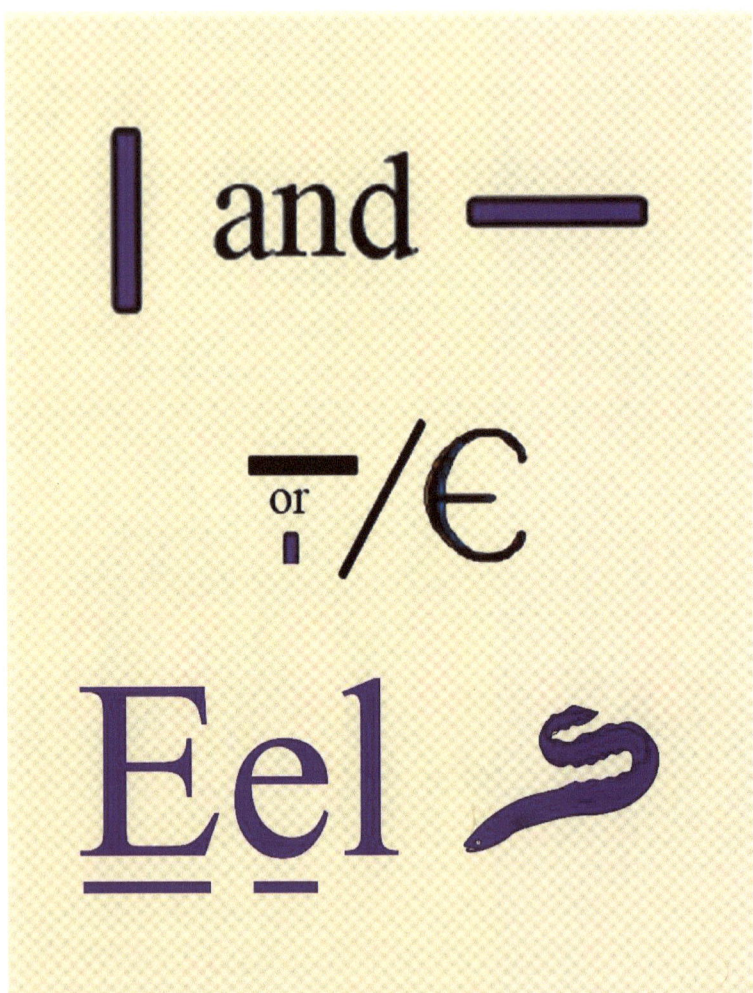

F f

Flag

G or G

G g

Goat

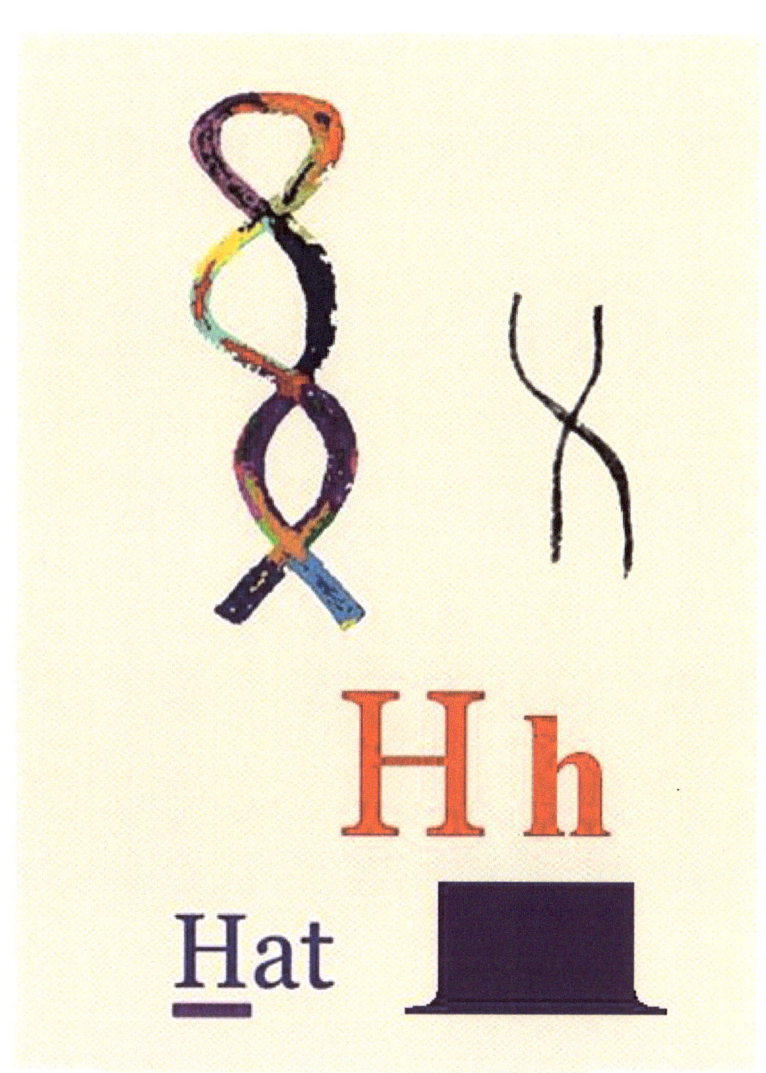

H h

Hat

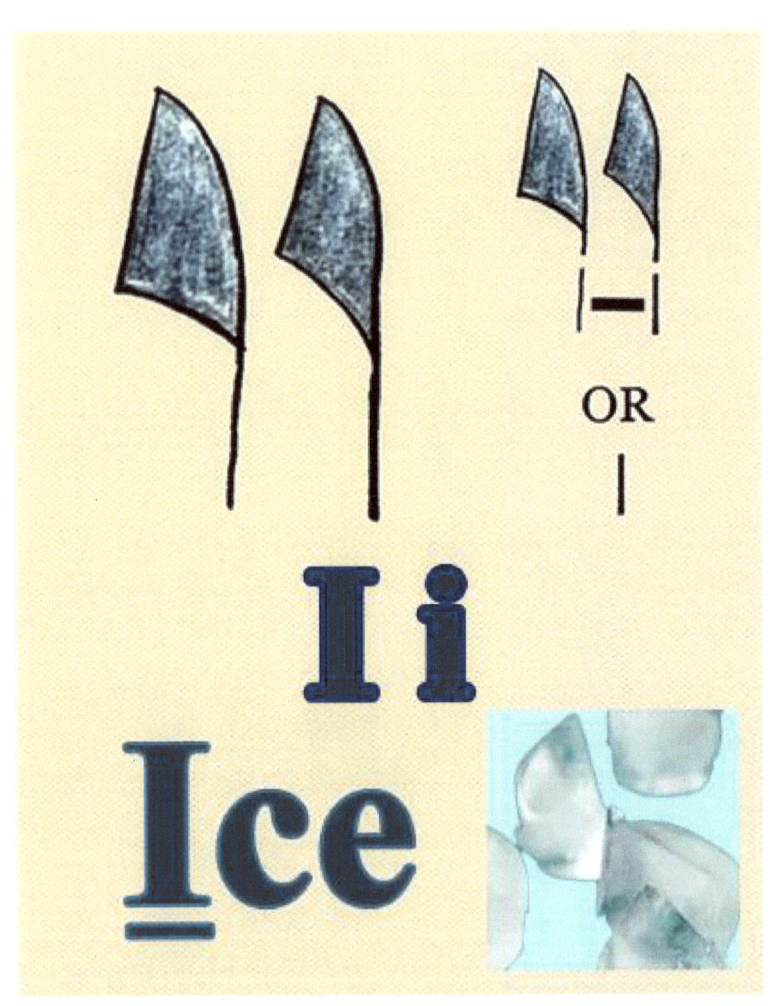

I i
Ice

K

Kite

L l
Lioness

Mountains

Pp
Peas

Q q

Question?

Tt
hot

Wood

X
Xenogamy

Yy
Yoyo

Z

Zebra

ABCs - 7000+ Years of EVOLUTION Worldwide

SESH MTUNTR Hieroglyphics 3500+ BCE	SESH SHA HIERATIC 3200+ BCE	SESH SHA II DEMOTIC 2000+ BCE	MetNi REM CHEMI COPTIC 1500+ BCE	KANANA/CANAAN PHOENICIAN 1500+ BCE	RASNA ETRUSCAN 1000+ BCE	UINE HELLENE GREEK 750+ BCE	Ha piru/IVRIT HEBREW 135-CE	AL ARABYAH ARABIC 650-CE	L' LATIN/LATIN ENGLISH 1000+ BCE
🦅	𐤀	ꝺ	Λa	𐤀	𐤀	Αα	א or אַ	١	A a
𓃀	𓃀	ƅ	Bß	𐤁	𐤁	Bβ	בּ	ب	B b
𓊪	𓊪	Σ	C	𐤂	𐤂	Σσ	ד	س	C
⌒	⌒	⌒	Δδ	𐤃	𐤃	Δδ	ד	د	D d
| and —	| and —	Jinkim Xникш	τ/Є	𐤄	𐤄	Εε	אָ	غ	E e
𓆓	𓆓	𓆓	Чq	𐤅	𐤅	Φφ	ף	ف	F f
𓎼 or G	𓎼	𓎼	Ƨ τ	𐤆	𐤆	Γγ	ג	ح	G g
*1	▲	Ꮣ	Γ-ʑ	Г-В	Ↄ-В	Γ-ξ	ח	ع	G-h
𓉔	𓉔	𓉔	S	𐤈	𐤈	Ξξ	ח	ح	H-h
\\\\	\\\\	\\\\	Iι	|	|	Iι	א	\	I i
𓐍	𓐍	𓐍	Χ	|	|	Υυ	י	ج	J j
▲	ꭓ	ꭓ	Κ	𐤊	𐤊	Κ	כ	ك	K k
𓃬	𓃬	Ⅼ	λ	𐤋	𐤋	Λλ	ל	ل	L l
𓅓	𓅓	𓅓	Μμ	𐤌	𐤌	Μμ	מ	م	M m
𓈖	𓈖	𓈖	Nn	𐤍	𐤍	Nν	נ	ن	N n
𓂀	𓂀	𓂀	O	O	O	O	א	ف	O
■	𓊪	𓊪	Ππ	𐤐	𐤐	Ππ	פ	ب	P p
𓃻	𓃻	𓃻	ϭ ϭ	𐤒	𐤒	Ϙ	ק	ق	Q q
◯	𓂋	𓂋	Pp/Ꝑ	𐤓	𐤓	Ρρ	ר	ر	R r
𓂋	𓂋	Ɛ	ϛ ϛ̄	𐤔	𐤔	Σσ	ש	س	S
𓎛	𓏏	Τ†	Ττ†	𐤕	𐤕	Ττ	ת	ت	T t
𓅉	𓅉	/	Υγ	V	V	Υ	ו	و	U u
𓂻\\	LL\\	ᛉ/\	Ββ	𐤐	𐤐	Ββ	ב	ق	V
𓃀	𓃀 or 𓃀	𓃀	Ⅲω	W	W	ω	ו	ف	W
𓀔	𓀔	𓀔	X	X	X	X	סד	كس	X
𓋴	𓋴	𓋴	Н	Y	Y	Υυ	א	غ	Y y
𓋴	𓋴	𓋴	Υγ	Y	Y	Υυ	י	غ	Y y
—	𓏲	𓏲	Ζz	𐤆	𐤆	Ζζ	ז	ذ, ظ	Z

© 2022 RICH AMENINHAT

Appendix

Page IX:

Discussion:

- What is the difference between Alphabet and ABCs?
- What is the difference in Alphabet and an alphabet?

Exercise:

- Find the definitions for each.

Fun Facts:

- Alphabet is named after two letters of the Coptic (Supposedly "last" writing of Ancient Egypt), Alpha and Bida, later pronounced Alpha Beta, *AlphaBet.*

Page 8:

Discussion:

- What is the difference between Planet and World?

Exercise:

- Discuss and find definitions. Note the physical traits of Astronomy, Topography and Geography

Fun Facts:

- If the planet was flat, it would have a linear start and end.
- Because it is round, like stars and moons, traveling it follows a circle which "revolves" infinitely.

Page 12:

Discussion:

- Who is Hansel and Gretel? What are their breadcrumbs and why are they so important to life lessons?

Exercise:

- Research the story. Perhaps change the Witch to a bad person who steals children.

Fun Facts:

- Child kidnapping and enslavement exists today in America and all around the world.
- We can be better citizens by being aware, keeping our children aware and safe and doing whatever we can to combat such things.

Page 16:

Discussion:

- Why did Russia get an Alphabet so late in history?

Exercise:

- Explore the history of Russia.

Fun Facts:

- Russian language is part of the Cyrillic grouping.
- The Russian language was revolutionized by an African-Russian man Ivan Pushkin, "The Father of Russian Literature."

Page 16:

Discussion:

- What is the youngest alpabet based on ABCs?
- How long ago was 800 CE?
- What is the difference between CE and AD?

Exercise:

- Research and Discussion.

Fun Facts:

- CE or Common Era is a scientifically accepted term related to History, Archeology, Anthropology, etc.

Page 18:

Discussion:

- What is PE (Present Era)?
- What is BPE (Before Present Era)?
- What are the differences between PE, CE and AD, and BPE, BCE, BC? What are some advantages or disadvantages of each?

Exercise:

- Research and Discussion.

Fun Facts:

- PE is a more modern, more objective based label for accounting historically objective time periods. The term has no overt or covert basis in religion, nor any specific bias perspectives or organizational afiliations

Page 20:

Discussion:

- Why are people not sure when Coptic came about?

Exercise:

- Research

Fun Facts:

- Coptic call themselves: Ni Rem Chemi Christiano.
- Coptic call Ancient Egyptians: Rem Chemi.
- The Coptic and Ancient Egyptian people originally come from the same area of the world: North African Egypt, Sudan, Ethiopia and the Horn of Africa, all the way south to the Great Lakes, Lake Nyanza (Lake Victoria), the extent of the Nile River.

Page 24:

Discussion:

- How did the Coptic, original Christians, develop from Chemit?
- What stories from Chemit parallel the Coptic's?
- Did other religions come directly from Chemit?

Exercise:

- Research and discussion

Fun Facts:

- The British museum has artifacts from Chemit (Ancient Egypt) and Punt (Ancient Sudan) going back to 10, 000 BCE.

Page 25:

Discussion:

- What does directly related mean relative to Chemit and Coptic?

Exercise:

- Research

Fun Facts:

- Another name for Coptic is *Bida* or *Beta Christian.*

Page 25:

Discussion:

- What does the name Chemit mean?
- What are other spellings of Chemit?
- How does it relate to the words Chemistry, Alchemy, Chemicals?

Exercise:

- Research and Discussion

Fun Facts:

- Though early (1800s) written that Chemit means black by Wallis Budge and later others, The people of Chemit, Chemau, left pictures of their skin color on walls and papyr (Papyrus paper from where the word paper comes). They ranged from the lightest to dark brown.
- The word Chem also means: *To burn,* as in to darken by burning.
- The Chemau left in their record that they are descendants of more southern Punt (Ancient Sudan) and darker skinned people.
- The Chemau left stories of the Nile River and people from Punt being from the Great Lakes region of Africa, Nyansa (Lake Victoria).

Page 26:

Discussion:

- What are the breadcrumbs of the Rosetta stone?
- What does Hieratic, Demotic and Coptic have to do with Linguistic breadcrumbs?

Exercise:

- Research and Discussion

Fun Facts:

- Chemit purposely left traces of their language from the development of Hieroglyphics to Hieratic to Demotic to Coptic because they knew it did and would serve as a teaching tool later.

Page 28:

Discussion:

- Who was Jean François Champollion?
- Why could no one for thousands of years do what he did?
- How did Champollion decipher the Rosetta Stone?
- Why did he not like the Academic Institutions so much?

Exercise:

- Research
    - The Linguist and the Emperor: Napoleon and Champollion's Quest to Decipher the Rosetta Stone
    - Cracking the Egyptian Code: The Revolutionary Life of Jean-Francois Champollion
    - *HD...* by Rich Ameninhat

Fun Facts:

- Champollion, other than assistance from his family and friends, was Self-Taught Coptic and other languages.
- Champollion was the first person in about 1800 years to decipher Ancient Egyptian Hieroglyphics.

Page 30:

Discussion:

- Has English and other languages ever been shown to be directly from Ancient Egyptian Hieroglyphics?
- How can Hieroglyphics help us better understand English and language in general?

Exercise:

- Research and Discussion

Fun Facts:

- For many years various people have suggested a direct link between Hieroglyphics and English, but no one has ever shown precise, factual, irrefutable detail of how; until about 5 years ago in this graph
- The graph came about from teaching my then 4-year-old daughter, Kylene Tiraet, how to write Hieroglyphics
- Kylene's middle name Tiraet is taken from the Chemit name Raet, meaning in Chemit and Etruscan: *She who writes*

Page 32:

Discussion:

- Why do Coptic and Greek look so much alike?
- Where did the Greeks get their Mythological stories?
- Who, What, When, Where, Why, How (5W-H) did Greece originate?

Exercise:

- 5W-H the origin of Greece
    - <u>African Presence in Early Europe</u> by Ivan Van Sertima
    - <u>Not Out of Greece</u> by Dr. Ra Un Nefer Amen
    - <u>HD…</u> by R. Ameninhat

Fun Facts:

- The story of Romulus, Remus and their mother as a She-Wolf is a fairytale to describe the origin of Greece.
- The story has clues of what really happened.

Page 34:

Discussion:

- Why do so many cultures have the same names for the letters of their Alphabet?
- What other cultural languages have the same or similar (*Samular*) names for their Alphabet?

Exercise:

- Research
    - <u>HD Hieroglyphic Definitives</u> by R. Ameninhat

Fun Facts:

- All "major"/most known religions in the world use the Ancient Egyptian Amen (Amen-Ra) as part of their prayers.

Page 36:

Discussion:

- Who is Gesenius?
- What does his book about Hebrew Grammar and his graph teach?

Exercise:

- Research and Discussion

Fun Facts:

- The origin for Hebrew that Gesenius shows on his chart is directly related to Phoenician and Etruscan ABCs, thus also developed from Hieroglyphics.

Page 38:

Discussion:

- What does older and younger mean in relation to Chemit and Phoenicia?

Exercise:

- Discussion

Fun Facts:

- Phoenicia was a City-State of Chemit several times in history and often paid monetary and spiritual respect to Chemit.
- The word Phoenicia means purple.
- Phoenicia is the word from which phoenix, phonics, phone and others like them originated
- The Phoenix is a story created from the Chemau story of *Bennu*, a sacred bird.
- Phoenicia is directly connected to North Africa, only separated by "man-made" canals (Suez) and such.
- Ancient Egyptians on record historically traveled as far as China, Russia and more
- The so-called continents of Africa and Asia and Europe are actually one connected land mass
- All land on Earth is connected under water, even islands; that's why islands stay in one spot, don't float around from place to place.

Page 41:

Discussion:

- What does the letter M mean in the Chemitic language?

Exercise:

- Research and Discussion

Fun Facts:

- The letter M in the Chemitic language is an Owl
- How owls act has a lot to do with the Chemitic meaning of the letter.

Page 42:

Discussion:

- What does the letter Q mean in the Chemitic language?

Exercise:

- Research and Discussion

Fun Facts:

- The Chemitic Q looks like a cup or bowl with a handle
- It is often miss taken as a K as in Kwanza, but in the Chemitic language similar sounding letters have different meanings.

Page 43:

Discussion:

- Why has it taken so long for the connection between ABCs to be made?
- What are other alphabets that look like ABC?

Exercise:

- Research and Discussion

Fun Facts:

- The link between ABCs can help a person learn several languages all at once.
- It helped the author be able to read and understand 9 or more different languages.

Page 45:

Discussion:

- What problems do people have with reading "my" letter chart?

Exercise:

- Discussion
- Spread the word

Fun Facts:

- The chart is a one of a kind meant to help revolutionize the acquisition and use of language.